Work At Home Jobs For Nurses & Other Healthcare Professionals

---

JANE JOHN-NWANKWO, RN, MSN, PHN

Work At Home Jobs For Nurses & Other Healthcare Professionals

Copyright © 2013 by Jane John-Nwankwo. RN, MSN

ISBN-13: 978-1491232033

ISBN-10: 149123203X

Printed in the United States of America

Dedication

Dedicated to all healthcare professionals who love their jobs but wishes to work from home part-time or full-time.

OTHER TITLES FROM THE SAME AUTHOR:

1. How to Make a Million in Nursing

2. Jokes for Nurses

3. Director of Staff Development: The Nurse Educator

4. Crisis Prevention & Intervention in Healthcare: Management of Assaultive Behavior

5. EKG Technician Study Guide

6. CNA Exam Prep: Nurse Assistant Practice Test Questions. Vol. One & Volume Two

7. The Home Health Aide Exam Prep

8. IV Therapy & Blood Withdrawal Review Questions

9. Choosing a Healthcare Career

10. EKG Test Prep

11. Phlebotomy Test Prep

Preface

"I work four to six days a week, 12 hour shifts and make $350 to $550 per shift, but I realize that I just have enough to pay all my bills with nothing left as I look forward to the next paycheck. I go for extra shifts, but that does not help, worst still I end up not having time for myself and not even staying in the house I am paying for. I would like to make some money on my days off working some few hours from my computer, or better still go full time working from home" If the above statement sounds like you, the answer is found in this book.

-Author

Introduction

Accepting the fact that a good number of individuals make money from home simply working from their computers and their phones encourages you to join a group that has the success secrets already and tap from the resources they already use. This book is designed to be interactive. Following the principles of this book will help you to be financially free, while still doing what you love.

-Jane John-Nwankwo RN, MSN

Idea 1: Healthcare Recruiting: Healthcare recruiting offers nurses the ability to step outside of the hospital and clinical setting into a role that will allow you to tap into your training and experience as a nurse while giving you the opportunity to put your high levels of energy and sales-driven mind to good work.

In the field of healthcare recruiting, one will essentially have the ability to set one's own salary as a fair amount of it shall be commission based, and it will be based upon the goals that you set for yourself. Do not be leery of the concept of a commission based position, as it will also come with a base salary that could be determined from where you live and on the company that you are working for. The healthcare field is an ever-expanding field so there will definitely not be a shortage of your skills and your abilities to recognize a good candidate for the job you are looking to fill.

Your Job Duties: In your role as a healthcare recruiter, you will work diligently to find qualified candidates to fill open healthcare positions. As a healthcare recruiter, you will obtain requirements from the hospital or practice that has the open position and you will then market the job opportunity to qualified healthcare professionals. Your job would be to pre-qualify the candidates interested in the position, based upon their credentials, their education, and the experience that they have within the field. You would also need to assist with coordinating the interview, and ensure that your candidates are well-prepared for their interviews.

Options for Recruiting Opportunities

Working as a healthcare recruiter will present you with several types of opportunities to choose from. The following are some of the options available:

- You could find employment working as an in-house recruiter for a healthcare facility, company, or hospital.

Your job will be to fill internal positions with the best qualified candidates for the job.

- You could find employment working for a recruiting agency. Your job will be to work with a variety of healthcare facilities, companies, or hospitals as you manage their searches for qualified candidates. You would be compensated for your services as a recruiter, and receive a 'finder's fee' once your candidate is hired by the facility.

- You start your own nurse staffing agency. Your job will be to seek out medical professionals who are interested in being contracted out, on an hourly basis, for short-term positions or substitute positions at a variety of healthcare facilities. For example, if a physician is out on vacation or maternity leave then your candidate will fill the open position until the absent physician returns to his or her position.

Healthcare recruiters are an essential part of the healthcare industry as their experience in the field as healthcare professionals will help to guide their decision-making processes, and help them to ensure that only the best candidates are considered for the jobs they are recruiting for.

Accomplishing Your Goals of $100,000 in 12 Months: Working on a commission basis will allow you to set your own goals and determine how much money you want to earn in this position. When you successfully place a candidate in a position, you should expect to receive 20% of the annual salary package that your candidate receives. Consider this scenario as a means of understanding how you can quickly reach your goals as a recruiter. You successfully place a registered nurse within a position at an area hospital. His or her annual salary is $65,000. The contract you agreed upon with the hospital states that your commission for finding them this exceptionally qualified candidate will be 15% of the registered nurse's salary. For a salary of $65,000 then you could expect to earn a commission of $9750. Now, of course, if you are working for a recruiting agency then they will take their own percentage of what you earn, but at the very minimum you should keep 60% of your commission.

That should put $5850 in your pocket, for the placement of one candidate. If you run on those numbers alone, and bear in mind that they could be significantly higher for some nursing positions and even for placement of physicians, you could easily earn $100,000 with the placement of 18 candidates. In the case that the recruiting firm is yours, which is the purpose of this book, realizing your goal of $100,000 in 12 months is less than 18 candidates. For an individual who is incredibly driven and excels at managing their time, healthcare recruiting can be a very lucrative experience for a nurse to work in.

Your expenses could include gas mileage, lunches and dinners with candidates and hiring companies, but they will all typically be tax-deductible as a part of your business expenses.

Idea 2: Medical writer

If you have a flair for creativity or the ability to translate medical components into a simplified language that is easy for the layperson to understand, then transitioning from a nurse working side-by-side with patients to a medical writer is just the career move for you. Your experience working in the healthcare field will put you in a prime position to understand the often complex medical terminology, while your writing skills can help you to write material that is easy for the reader to easily understand.

Your Job Duties: Because medical writing can encompass a wide range of work completed for media, industry, government and pharmaceutical companies, your job duties could vary greatly from one position to the next.

- You may be required to investigate and research findings about new products and new drugs and then prepare documents that will be used to seek approval from the FDA.

- You could find yourself helping physicians with writing their research papers or medical reviews.

- You may work with continuing medical education companies that develop educational materials to help medical professionals prepare for the next phase of continuing their education and furthering their career.

- You could find work writing about new and exciting research developments for medical journals, magazines, newspapers, websites, and other publications that offer a focus on healthcare issues.

Your hands-on experience as a healthcare professional will put you in a great position to understand how the medical and healthcare industry works.

Options for Medical Writer Opportunities

As a healthcare professional with exceptional writing skills you will find yourself very much in demand at a number of companies. Some of the places that you could find yourself working on your way to accomplishing your goal of earning $100,000 a year include the following.

- Pharmaceutical companies

- Medical software firms

- Medical device manufacturers

- Universities and other continuing education companies

- Clinical research organizations

- Government organizations with a focus on healthcare

- Medical journals

- Medical websites

- Freelance writing

- Authoring books for renowned publishing companies

- Independent publishing (which is one of the things I do)

- Ghostwriting for non-academic papers where the author has the idea of what to write but lacks the writing ability. The price is usually $20 to $50 for every 250 words (a page). In an 8 hour day, while making your lunch and taking necessary breaks from your home computer, you can type up nothing less than 10 pages.

If your charge was $40/page, that would be $400 a day. If you do this 10 days on your days-off in a month, you have $4000 in your hands outside your paycheck. As your name is known and the published authors use you as repeat customers while you are still securing more clients, you can start outsourcing your job to other seasoned writers. Many professional ghostwriters make a minimum of $20,000 a month working from home. Please make sure that your services are not used for academic purposes. A good way to start freelance writing will be enrolling in websites like elance.com and other such sites for freelance writing, advertising your services under classifieds, writing to medical and nursing journals, etc. Whether you are writing presentations, research papers, or technical manuals for medical devices, there are a number of key skills that you will need to have in order to find success in your new field. You will need to have the ability to translate healthcare studies into an approachable language that is

16

custom-tailored to reach out to the targeted audience. This could involve translating a particular complex medical study into several different versions that are appropriate for healthcare professionals, investors, regulators, or even the general public. There will be need to have good attention to detail, be flawless in your accuracy, have exceptional research skills, and of course, possess solid writing talents

Accomplishing Your Goals of $100,000 in 12 Months:
The medical writer is not often thought of as being a lucrative career choice. But the reality is that an accomplished writer with good credentials as a nurse will be in a position to command a much higher income. You may need to get a few jobs in order to establish yourself as a subject matter expert, but with a good writing portfolio and the drive to succeed in your chosen career, you could easily land yourself into making between $5,000 to $20,000 a month just writing from your computer for different companies, part-time.

The average salary for a medical writer in the USA sits at $75,000 but it can easily be improved upon by ensuring that your writing skills are exceptional and that your nursing and medical knowledge skills are without fault. The larger pharmaceutical companies are also often very generous with the salaries they offer to their medical writers. Keeping up with current medical advances and writing your own editorials for submission in healthcare publications are great ways to boost your income.

Whether you are working as a medical writer for the top medical schools in the country or publishing research articles in notable medical journals, or even publishing your own books like you have mine in your hands, you are sure to find out that being a medical writer is a hugely fulfilling career opportunity without a paid office.

Idea 3: Healthcare Education

With the rate that the healthcare field is expanding, there are endless opportunities for a talented and experienced nurse with exceptional credentials to step into the position of being a nurse educator. This will give you the ability to continue working in the healthcare field while helping to shape the next generation of healthcare professionals who will be responsible for patient care. If you are thinking in this realm, you will benefit from my book called "Director of Staff Development: The Nurse Educator"

While there may be some additional educational steps required in order for you to be well-qualified for the position, working in healthcare education can be one of the most rewarding corners of the healthcare field to step into. The good part is that you can teach from your computer from any location in the world. How do you start? Depending on the level of your education as a nurse, submit as many online applications to online healthcare institutions.

Job Duties As A Healthcare Educator: As a healthcare educator you would have a variety of job responsibilities as you conduct the different-level courses in the healthcare field, ranging from simple CPR or BLS classes to degree awarding courses. You will be responsible for the preparation and the delivery of lectures, as well as responsible for leading and engaging in classroom discussions with your nursing students.

Other responsibilities include administering and grading exams, helping students with issues they appear to be struggling with and hands-on clinical classes. There will be the need to have a solid familiarity with the best nursing practices and procedures, while still keeping up with technological advances.

Healthcare educators often embark on their own research projects and publish their findings in medical journals.

This can give you great opportunity for making a name for yourself in the field, and also help you on the right track toward achieving your financial goals.

Options for Healthcare Educator Opportunities: The commonest choice for you to seek out a position as a healthcare educator will be at area universities and community colleges. It is important to note that you will be able to command a much higher salary if you work at a larger university within a larger metropolitan area.

But if you do not have all the credentials yet, with your nursing license, you can apply to the board of nursing to approve the courses you have written for continuous education and that is the best place to start. That is in fact, where I started.

When you start teaching the continuous education classes, you will look into what it takes to teach a class at a bigger school. Educate yourself, take the course, and apply for the job and get the experience which you may use to apply to your own school as it grows. It is always good to start low but with great plans, learning and dropping mistakes along the way. If you do not wish to start your own school, you can teach for other companies.

A large number of hospital networks offer their own nurse training programs and require experienced healthcare educators to step in and provide their students with the hands-on experience that will ensure they are prepared to take charge of patient care.

Accomplishing Your Goals of $100,000 in 12 Months: In the United States the average professor of nursing can expect to command a salary of $85,000. In order to achieve your goals of $100,000 in 12 months, you can take a job as an online instructor while you have time to grow your business.

You will need to ensure that you are the leader in your field. This can be accomplished by ensuring that you have extensive knowledge of the latest healthcare technology advances and that you have the leadership qualities that will help you to stand head and shoulders above others in your field. I have friend that has two jobs as an online instructor. He has all the time in his hands, takes vacation all the time and commands his full salary of about $80,000 from each school. The healthcare educators of today are shaping the healthcare providers of tomorrow and the best universities, community colleges, and independent schools are typically willing to pay for the privilege of hiring qualified nurse educators.

Many LVNs do not know that they can teach fellow LVNs in their clinical rotations. Check your state requirements and discover the gold in your hands that you never knew you had.

With a minimal investment of your time and by taking the classes and certifications that will put you in the top of your field, you will be able to easily command a salary of at least $130,000 in 12 months.

Idea 4: Legal Nurse Consultant

While working as a nurse has its own set of rewards, working as a legal nurse consultant is one of the better career moves that can help you to achieve your goals of earning $100,000 in 12 months. As a legal nurse consultant, your knowledge of the healthcare field can help you to provide expert opinions and testimony on legal cases that have some medical significance. This means that you would be working in conjunction with a team of legal professionals on cases that could be groundbreaking or even life-changing for those who are involved in them. With specialized training that will give you a good knowledge of the way in which the law works, you will be ready to work side-by-side with attorneys in order to achieve results for their clients.

Job Duties as a Legal Nurse Consultant

While you may not need extensive training as a legal nurse consultant, you will still be working with enough details about the law to need a firm grasp of medical law. By using your experience and your expertise as a healthcare professional you will be consulting with clients, closely reading all of their medical records, understanding and explaining often complex medical terminology, and giving your expert opinion on a range of healthcare issues. Your primary responsibility will be to effectively bridge the gap in medical knowledge that attorneys will have.

The attorneys that you will work with will be the legal experts and you will play the role of the expert in the healthcare system and on the nursing profession. You will need to screen cases to determine whether there is a legal merit in them, assist the attorneys and paralegals with the process of discovery, conduct extensive medical research, closely review patient medical records, identify the standards of care that patients received, prepare your own reports, provide evidence, and you may also need to act as an expert witness, or help to locate those who can provide expert testimony. As a legal nurse consultant you will play a vital role in ensuring a fair outcome in a number of legal issues. You will be a vital part of the legal team that you work with, and you will be well compensated for your expertise.

Options for Legal Nurse Consultant Opportunities

There are a large number of opportunities for legal nurse consultants to find employment that will help them to meet their financial goals.

- Law firms are naturally the first place to consider for finding employment as a legal nurse consultant, especially those that specialize in medical-related class action suits and other types of medical lawsuits.

- There is also the potential to find employment working in select government agencies that relate to medical law and medical regulations.

- Insurance companies regularly hire legal nurse consultants in order to help with lawsuits or the potential for legal issues. Working for insurance companies and HMOs could be a very lucrative position to consider.

- Hospitals, especially larger hospital networks, routinely hire on legal nurse consultants to work in their risk management department. With knowledge of medical law and excellent nursing credentials, you'll be in a good position to help hospitals understand what their risks and obligations are when legal issues are concerned.

Accomplishing Your Goals of $100,000 in 12 Months:

The average salary of a legal nurse consultant in the United States is about $200,000 a year. With the right certifications and credentials under your belt, you could easily add more to your $200,000 a year with other businesses you can set up all within 12 months.

Working as an independent contractor can allow you much more in the way of freedom and flexibility, and if you are already a respected legal nurse consultant then you could command an hourly rate of $200 an hour.

With a bit of time taken to obtain the relevant certifications and time taken to learn more about medical law, you will easily be able to earn the salary that will help to ensure all of your financial goals are being met.

Idea 5: Medical consulting: As a medical consultant you will be able to call on your medical training to provide solid medical advice for a variety of situations and purposes. Your experience working as a nurse and your credentials will give you the ability to be very knowledgeable about many facets of the medical community, current medical procedures and medical facts. You will work as an advisor to provide custom-tailored help and advice to the healthcare community in order to meet the complex needs of the practices that you are working for.

Job Duties As A Medical Consultant: The type of job responsibilities that you have could vary greatly based upon the company that you are working for, and also on the experience that you have personally. A medical consultant is typically hired in order to review books and medical publications in order to verify the accuracy of medical facts, and also to make suggestions for changes that could improve the quality of the writing. You may also review scripts for movies or television in order to provide expertise opinions on the plotlines and proposed medical situations. Your job as a medical consultant could have you assisting doctors with the process of setting up their own private practice, recruit medical staff, help to design the layout of the medical facility, and also review advertisements for medical products, medical services, and medical facilities.

Medical consultants often spend time analyzing how a medical practice is operated in order to ensure that the practice is operating efficiently and profitably.

Any project that could require the input of a medical professional will find you putting your experience and knowledge to the test.

Options for Medical Consulting Opportunities

There are a great number of opportunities for medical consultants to find excellent salaried positions, through a variety of medical practices and private companies.

- Script writers
- Medical writers
- Movie and television studios
- Hospitals
- Medical facility planners
- Medical product manufacturers
- Private practices setting up new facilities
- Law firms
- Insurance companies, both health and automobile

With a proven track-record in the medical field, the nurse is able to secure a position as a medical consultant in no time at all. If working for another company even as a contractor does not appeal to you then you could consider going into business for yourself. A private medical consultant with an established reputation could find themselves involved in an incredible amount of business in a relatively short amount of time. There would be a fair amount of marketing and business promotion required, so it could be beneficial to take some marketing and business courses as needed.

Accomplishing Your Goals of $100,000 in 12 Months:
As a medical consultant your skills will be much in demand as companies, writers, insurance agencies and physicians strive to ensure that they are operating as efficiently and as profitably as possible. The average salary for a medical consultant in the United States is $90,000. This means that there is a great potential for expansion and salary growth. Within a few very short months you can use your on-the-job experience as a medical consultant, combined with your nursing credentials and business savvy to rapidly increase your salary so that you are easily commanding a salary of $100,000. If you go into business for yourself as an independent consultant, you have the potential for

unlimited income as your business grows in leaps and bounds. With a minimal investment in some marketing and business management courses you will have a solid idea as to how to best run your business and market your skills. Not only will these courses be tax deductible but they are an excellent investment towards meeting your financial goals. You can also run a medical consultant agency where you employ other nurses to work for you.

Idea 6: Athletic consultant

Sports medicine is a very interesting niche market that could prove to be hugely rewarding, fulfilling, and of course really lucrative. Working as an athletic consultant, you could find yourself working directly with athletes, directly with insurance companies, or with a range of other healthcare or athletic professionals. Your experiences working in the healthcare field will provide you with the hands-on knowledge that will be resourceful as an athletic consultant.

It will be very beneficial to have a good working knowledge of sports medicine so that you can best serve your patients and also command a higher salary due to the combination of your experience and your education.

Job Duties As An Athletic Consultant

The on the job duties of an athletic consultant could vary greatly, based upon the type of company that you are working for. Some of the day-to-day duties you face could include the following:

- Measuring the overall health status of athletes
- Diagnosing minor injuries and also offering treatment for minor injuries
- Checking vital signs and monitoring for fluctuations that could indicate the potential for a problem
- Writing reports and determining the eligibility of athletes for certain programs and jobs

You could find yourself working very much in a hands-on position with the athletes you meet with, or you could simply be monitoring their medical charts to determine whether their medical history has cause for alarm. Your job duties could be as varied as the types of sports that you could be involved with.

Options for Athletic Consulting Opportunities: As an athletic consultant, you will truly be working in a niche market that doesn't offer perhaps as many opportunities as other nursing opportunities will. However,

there are still plenty of great job openings for an individual with a proven track-record and the needed training and experience to become a leading expert in the field of athletic consultancy. The following are just some of the sources of employment opportunities for athletic consultants.

• Professional sporting teams, in the NFL, NBA, etc. These types of teams routinely hire on athletic consultants to help them determine the overall health of the players that they are considering recruiting, and to help provide treatment for minor injuries or ailments when needed. You may find that this position is not only incredibly lucrative but also gives you the opportunity to travel with the team.

- Universities with sports teams, particularly the larger universities, will routinely use the services of athletic consultants to help them determine whether new players are in excellent physical health, and to also treat their players for minor issues that could otherwise keep them from playing their best.

- Insurance companies that hold policies on serious sporting competitors will frequently use athletic consultants to evaluate the health and medical claims of the athletes that may be making claims against the policies. It will then be up to you to determine the validity of the claim.

Private consulting, where you go into business for yourself, will offer you the ability to take on patients on an individual basis. You may also find yourself with contracts with area universities and minor league sports teams.

Accomplishing Your Goals of $100,000 in 12 Months:

The bigger the company or university that you work with, the bigger salary you will be able to command.

Landing a position with one of the larger sporting teams can be incredibly lucrative and easily see you attaining your financial goals. This is not possible for everyone however, so you may find that going into business for yourself is your best course of action.

By actively promoting your skills and services as an athletic consultant, you will be able to quickly build up a solid network of contacts and soon be well on your way toward your goal of earning $100,000 in 12 months. You may also need to hire the services of a marketing firm to help you develop your brand, but it will be an investment well worth considering as you sit back and watch your dreams of financial stability come to fruition.

Idea 7 Quality improvement (consulting)

As a quality improvement consultant you will be able to put your extensive experience in the nursing field to good use as you help healthcare facilities, medical professionals, drug manufacturers, and others in the healthcare field to improve their product quality, their service quality, and to overall improve their potential for profitability. When you think about the time spent working with all of your patients day in and day out, you can likely think of several situations where the quality of patient care was just up to standard. Perhaps you made your opinions known to your supervisor or other hospital management. If the hospital that you were working for at the time had a quality improvement professional on board then there are good odds that the issues were investigated and remedied in order to improve the patient experience.

Job Duties As A Quality Improvement Professional:

You could find yourself performing a range of job duties that have you working directly with patients to best understand their experience,

or working with other healthcare professionals in order to determine whether their methods and practices are in the best interest of the patients and in the best interests of the healthcare facility. Some of the skills that you will need to have in order to succeed as a quality improvement professional include the following.

- A sharp understanding of clinical care and clinical processes
- Strong analytical abilities
- Leadership skills
- Organization and presentation skills
- Conflict resolution expertise
- Master knowledge of state and federal laws as are applicable to healthcare

- People management skills
- Budget management

The majority of quality improvement positions working in healthcare will have a large number of responsibilities that may fall into several types of categories. Some of the job duties that you could find yourself having could include the following.

- Training and education of hospital staff
- Evaluation and analysis of current practices
- Regulatory compliance
- Risk management
- Analyzing hospital and patient data for care trends
- Determining the root causes for negative trends associated with patient care
- Promoting good quality practices
- Creating new policies and procedures that are intended to improve the quality of patient care and reduce the risks of patient harm

41

The healthcare facility that you work for may also require that you oversee reports of patient care benchmarks and provide reports to federal and state authorities alike. Your position could have you juggling as many as a dozen projects at one time, all with the implicit goal of improving the type of care that patients are receiving.

Options for Quality Improvement Professionals

Opportunities: Working for a hospital or large group of hospitals is typically going to be the most common position for a quality improvement professional to find.

It is important to note that the larger the facility and the larger the metropolitan area, the larger the salary that you can command will be. You will also have the potential for working in extended care facilities and also short-term care facilities like rehabilitation centers and nursing homes. A lot of insurance companies also routinely hire quality improvement professionals so that they can be assured of providing their patients with the best possible care.

Accomplishing Your Goals of $100,000 in 12 Months:

The average salary for a quality improvement professional in the healthcare field, working in the United States, is $85,000 a year. While this salary does fall short of your goal of $100,000 a year you can quickly bring your salary up to better meet your financial goals by ensuring that you are the best candidate for the job. This can be accomplished by taking courses in business management, hospital management, patient care, and courses that relate to state and federal laws.

Another great option for easily seeing your financial goals attained is by going into business as a quality improvement consultant. This will allow you to spend time in a facility or even a private practice for just a few short weeks or months, carefully analyzing patient care and protocols. Your reputation is sure to grow swiftly and you will soon find yourself very easily realizing your goals of earning $100,000 in 12 short months.

Idea 8: Medical equipment sales

Medical equipment plays a vital role in the diagnosis of patient illnesses, and can also offer the solution in a variety of treatment options. The medical equipment used in hospitals and other healthcare facilities today is continually being redeveloped and improved upon in order to provide a better experience for the patient. The companies that manufacture live-saving medical equipment need sales representatives who will help them to market their products to healthcare providers within their territory and even in other cities and states. For a sales-oriented and goal-driven individual, this can be the perfect opportunity to put your experience and skills as a nursing professional to good use as you demonstrate the capabilities of the medical equipment that you are representing.

Job Duties of a Medical Equipment Sales

Representative: The position of a medical equipment sales representative is heavily commission based, which means that you will need to be highly driven, determined, and a little bit pushy in order to get your products seen and utilized by the medical professionals that you are meeting with each and every day. You will likely need to spend a fair amount of time traveling between medical facilities as you demonstrate your products, but you will also get to meet with a lot of people who can help you to continually expand your network and your reach. You will need to be completely informed about each of the features and functions of the medical devices that you are representing. You must be able to use the device well enough to demonstrate it in front of physicians, nurse practitioners, medical assistants, and other healthcare professionals.

This is a high-pressured sales position that can prove to be hugely lucrative for those who are willing to do their utmost to get their products seen, tested, and prove to have good sales closing skills.

Options for Medical Equipment Sales Representative Opportunities: There are a number of medical equipment manufacturers in the country that are constantly seeking motivated sales reps who have high levels of energy and positive attitudes about them. Your background in healthcare will have already familiarized you with a lot of the equipment that is already being used in hospitals, doctor's offices, and other clinic settings. Research the companies that you are most familiar with as this will give you an edge when you are marketing their products. After all, you are much more believable and reliable as a sales representative if you have actually experienced using those same products in a clinical setting and on patients.

Accomplishing Your Goals of $100,000 in 12 Months:

Medical equipment sales representatives will receive a fair amount of company perks and great

typically earn a modest base salary, but will also often

financial incentives for meeting their sales quotas. The base salary you earn will vary based on where you live, the size of the manufacturing company, and the type of products that you are representing. You could expect to see an average base salary of around $50,000, which essentially places you at the halfway mark toward earning your goal of $100,000. Keep in mind that a good quality product placed in front of the right medical professionals will essentially market and sell itself. The commission structure that you work with will be unique to the company that you are working for, but on average you can expect to see a

30% commission of the sale of the equipment that you are selling. This means that you can expect to see a commission of around $6000 for each piece of equipment that you are able to sell. Your quota for the year might be to sell 20 products, which means that if you hit the minimum of your quota you could be easily earning in excess of $100,000 in commission alone. A truly driven medical equipment sales representative can earn a very respectable living, which will put you well on your pathway toward financial stability and security.

Idea 9: Medical Insurance Sales Representative

As a nurse you likely experienced first-hand what a lack of appropriate medical insurance coverage could mean for your patients. Working as a medical insurance sales representative will allow you the opportunity to encourage your potential clients to purchase the medical insurance that will help to protect them in the event that they or a member of their family is in need of medical treatment.

This type of career choice is not always the idea choice for those who are transitioning out of a nursing career, but it can definitely come with the potential to earn a steady income that exceeds the financial goals that you have set for yourself.

Job Duties As A Medical Insurance Sales Representative

This type of position is typically very heavily commission based, which means that you will need to do your utmost to learn all there is to know about the various medical insurance packages that you are representing. You will need to know all about the benefits of the insurance and be able to convey your thoughts to your potential clients with a positive and assertive attitude. Having had experience encouraging patients to take their medication, you are sure to find that it is a breeze to encourage your clients to purchase medical insurance policies that will provide their families with adequate coverage.

Keep in mind that the policies you will be representing won't just incorporate standard medical care. They may also offer coverage for long-term health care and also potentially be related to short or long-term disability coverage insurance.

Options for Medical Insurance Sales Opportunities

There are dozens of companies offering a sales-oriented and goal-driven individual the ability to earn a really decent income. But how do you narrow down your choices so that you are selecting the right company?

First and foremost you should do extensive research into any company before you apply for employment with them. Learn as much as you can about their reputation and about the products that they are marketing. It could prove to be hugely disappointing to get hired with a company that simply doesn't offer good insurance packages and is also known for being simply a bad company to work with.

Be acutely aware of any companies that are asking for money upfront from you. In the typical medical insurance sales world you won't need to pay any money to a company that you are going to work for. Instead, the company will need to hire you on as a full-time employee, include a contract, and establish what your base commission for the position will be.

Accomplishing Your Goals of $100,000 in 12 Months

The average medical insurance sales person makes a base salary of $35,000 per year, in the United States. That might be a paltry figure when you consider that your goal is to earn a minimum of $100,000 in a 12 month period. However, there are a few things that you should consider. Medical insurance sales is very much a commission driven industry, which means that you have the potential to earn an average of 30% on top of each policy that you sell. The more policies that you sell, on top of your quota, the more commission that you will be able to earn, and the closer you will be to achieving your goal. Consider a moderately priced 6-month insurance policy of $1,000. It may not seem like very much, but your commission on that will be in the neighborhood of $300. Now consider the commission that you could see if you sell a mere 200 policies in a 12 month period.

That could net you a profit of $60,000, on top of your base salary. Naturally if you sell more policies and sell add-ons to each policy then you will be able to realize your goal of $100,000 in 12 months a lot sooner.

Idea 10: Quality Resource Director

The role of quality resource director will perform a variety of functions within a hospital or other types of healthcare facility. This job will call upon your training and experience as a healthcare provider and allow you to ensure that the best interests of the hospital, or healthcare facility, along with the patient's needs are being simultaneously met.

Job Duties As A Quality Resource Director

In your role as quality resource director, you will be responsible for overseeing the level of quality in the care that patients receive, as well as the appropriateness of the care that is being provided to the patient. This can help to ensure that the patients are not receiving medical treatment that they do not necessarily require in order to restore their good health and also help to protect the resources of the hospital.

As part of your duties you will also analyze the efficiency of current staff levels and make recommendations for either reassigning staff members or hiring on new staff members to improve patient care and staff efficiency.

You will need to review the admissions to the hospital and verify their need for continued treatment on an inpatient basis. By evaluating whether a patient truly needs to be in the hospital, you will also be able to make a determination on whether the type of treatment they will be receiving is the most appropriate course of treatment for their particular situation.

While physicians will have the final signoff, it will be in the best interests of the hospital to determine whether the resources truly need to be expended in that direction.

Options for Quality Resource Director Opportunities

Working within a hospital setting is one of the best places for you to find a position as a quality resource manager, but you may find working in a number of other healthcare facilities to be just as lucrative for you. Some of the other types of places you may find opportunities for quality resource management positions include the following.

- Extended care nursing facilities
- Physical and surgical recovery facilities
- Rehabilitation facilities
- Insurance companies
- Surgery centers

Many healthcare facilities are typically eager to promote from within, especially as it will ensure that they are putting decision makers in positions to make their decisions about the hospital, the staff, and the treatments that they are already familiar with.

Accomplishing Your Goals of $100,000 in 12 Months

The average salary of a quality resource director in the United States is $112,000 a year. This means that by working as a quality resource director you will be able to easily realize your goal of earning $100,000 in 12 months. You may need to consider taking on some business classes so that you will be well-equipped to combine your knowledge of healthcare with your newly acquired business acumen.

You may need to enter the field on a manager level, and then spend the next 6-12 months establishing your reputation within the industry. With experience under your belt you will easily be able to step into the director's position and see the salary increase that will help you to accomplish your goals of financial security.

In conclusion, below are listed 10 ways a nurse can make money online. I will elaborate on them in the next book:

1. A blog dealing with general nursing issues

Many people interested in nursing or those who are nurses already crave information concerning this career. You will have a lot of traffic when you are able to fill the information deficit for them through a well-kept blog.

2. Start a weight loss blog

There are several blogs dealing with weight loss and your experience as a nurse should be what makes you stand out.

Give the health dimensions of weight loss techniques and approaches. People will be grateful to have weight loss information given to them by an expert which means they can then be safer even as they try to shed extra pounds.

3. Blog about diet and nutrition

Diet and nutrition information is crucial to all people. When you avail information on this aspect for different groups of people and constantly refresh it, you will have a huge audience which finds your blog a great resource.

4. Write and Sell E-books online

The beauty about e-books is that for a 25-page document, one could make up to $30 per download. As far the imformation is needed and you have put down useful information to serve a hungry population, you will make money while you sleep!

5. Sell clothes, shoes and equipment generally needed by nurses

This is yet another way to make some good cash online.
When you have a proper delivery routine, nurses and
student nurses will be your loyal customers.

6. **Become a nurse instructor online**

You can instruct people online, especially student nurses.
Skills like CPR can also be taught in this manner and so
can high school science subjects.

7. **Multi-level marketing as concerns healthcare
   products**

This has become an important source of income for many
people and when you become active in the healthcare niche
given your nursing knowledge, you can really make the cut.
I make money through this, selling Aloe Vera and Bee
products. You can visit my website:

www.AloeVeraHealthAndWealth.com

8. **Offer nurse consultancy services via the internet**

This may involve a bit of travel and might even mean that you bring some more nurses on board. If this is not tenable, concentrate on services which can be given online. There are several nursing consultancy services which might not need travel on your part. Consultancy services for risk management, for example, can be comfortably given online.

9. **Write articles for healthcare related websites and blogs**

You will use your knowledge to provide websites and blogs with the necessary nursing-related articles. This can be handy for those who have little time to spend online.

10. **Medical transcription services**

If you have knowledge in nursing, you can quickly acquaint yourself with medical transcription training given your medical background. A certificate course, for example, may not take up much time but will be productive when you delve into provision of medical transcription services online.

OTHER TITLES FROM THE SAME AUTHOR:

1. Director of Staff Development: The Nurse Educator
2. Crisis Prevention & Intervention in Healthcare: Management of Assaultive Behavior
3. CNA Exam Prep: Nurse Assistant Practice Test Questions. Vol. One
4. CNA Exam Prep: Nurse Assistant Practice Test Questions. Vol Two
5. IV Therapy & Blood Withdrawal Review Questions
6. Medical Assistant Test Preparation
7. EKG Test Prep
8. Phlebotomy Test Prep
9. The Home Health Aide Textbook
10. Patient Care Technician Exam Review Questions
11. Acute Care Nurse Assistant Exam Prep
12. Home Health Aide Exam Prep

Order these books at
www.bestamericanhealthed.com/resources.html
Or call 951 637 8332 for bulk purchase

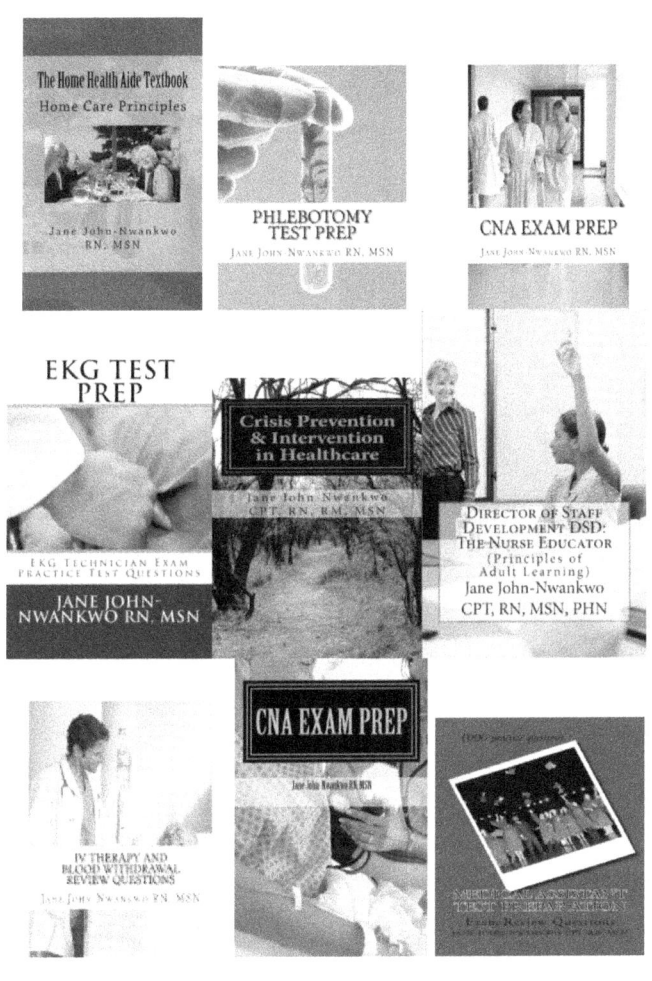

Order these books at
www.nurserapport.com/books.html

www.ingramcontent.com/pod-product-compliance
Lightning Source LLC
Chambersburg PA
CBHW071630170526
45166CB00003B/1270